Usborne First Experiences
Going to the Doctor

Anne Civardi

Illustrated by Stephen Cartwright

Edited by Michelle Bates
Cover design by Neil Francis

Medical adviser: Catherine Sims BSc; MBBS and Dr. Lance King

There is a little yellow duck hiding on every page. Can you find it?

This is the Jay family.

Mrs. Jay

Mr. Jay

Jack Jay

Jenny Jay

Joey Jay

Nod

Rory

Jenny has woken up with a bad cough and Jack has hurt his arm. They must go and see the doctor.

Mrs. Jay phones the doctor.

She makes an appointment while Mr. Jay helps Jack get dressed. "Ow," shouts Jack, "watch my arm, Dad."

The Jays go to see the doctor.

Mrs. Jay takes Jack, Jenny and Joey to see Doctor Woody.
"Our appointment is at 2 o'clock," she tells the receptionist.

The receptionist checks her book.

"Yes, it's for Jack and Jenny, isn't it?" she says. "And for Joey too," says Mrs. Jay. "He needs to have his immunization."

The Jays sit in the waiting room.

There are lots of people waiting to see the doctor. Mrs. Jay reads a book to Jenny. Jack and Joey want to play.

Now it is the Jays' turn.

Doctor Woody calls their name. "Who shall I see first?"
she says. "Me," says Jack, holding out his arm.

Doctor Woody examines Jack.

She looks at his sore arm. "It's not broken," she says, "but you do have a sprained wrist, Jack."

Doctor Woody puts Jack's arm in a sling.

"Just wear this for a few days," Doctor Woody tells him.
"It will feel better soon."

Doctor Woody checks Jenny.

She takes her temperature with a thermometer. Then she looks down Jenny's throat. "It's very red," she says.

Then she examines Jenny's ears with an otoscope. "Your ears are fine," she tells Jenny.

Doctor Woody listens to Jenny's breathing with a stethoscope. "Breathe in and out deeply," she says.

She feels Jenny's neck to see if her glands are swollen. "You have a slight chest infection," she says.

Jenny needs some medicine.

Doctor Woody prints a prescription for Jenny from her computer. Then she sits down at her desk and signs it.

Now it is Joey's turn.

Doctor Woody gives Joey his immunization. It only hurts a little.

She also gives Joey some drops so that he won't get polio. Then she says goodbye to the Jays.

*Sometimes you have an injection to stop you from getting polio.

The Jays pick up Jenny's prescription.

Mrs. Jay stops at the pharmacy. She gives the pharmacist the prescription and he gives her some medicine.

At home, Mrs. Jay puts Jenny to bed.

Mrs. Jay tucks Jenny in and gives her a spoonful of medicine. "You'll be better soon," she says.

That evening, Mr. Jay comes home from work.

"How are you all?" he says. Jack jumps to his feet. "Joey's all right, and Jenny's in bed," he says. "But look at my sling!"

This edition published in 2005 by Usborne Publishing Ltd, Usborne House, 83-85 Saffron Hill, London EC1N 8RT, England.
Copyright © 2005, 1992 Usborne Publishing Ltd. www.usborne.com
First published in America in 2005. UE
The name Usborne and the devices ♀ ⊕ are Trade Marks of Usborne Publishing Ltd.